S0-ABC-355

St Croix Falls Library
230 S Washington St
St Croix Falls WI 54024

VOLKSWAGEN

Cars People Love

Mason Crest

Mason Crest
450 Parkway Drive, Suite D
Broomall, PA 19008
www.masoncrest.com

© 2018 by Mason Crest, an imprint of National Highlights, Inc.

All rights reserved. No part of this publication may be reproduced or transmitted in any form or by any means, electronic or mechanical, including photocopying, recording, taping, or any information storage and retrieval system, without permission from the publisher.

Printed and bound in the United States of America.

Series ISBN: 978-1-4222-3963-6
Hardback ISBN: 978-1-4222-3968-1
EBook ISBN: 978-1-4222-7820-8

First printing
1 3 5 7 9 8 6 4 2

Additional text by John Perritano.
Cover photograph by Volkswagen of America Media Images.

Library of Congress Cataloging-in-Publication Data is on file with the publisher.

CARS 4
EVERYONE

CONVERTIBLES

DREAM CARS

MUSCLE CARS

SUVS

VOLKSWAGEN

QR CODES DISCLAIMER:

You may gain access to certain third party content ("Third-Party Sites") by scanning and using the QR Codes that appear in this publication (the "QR Codes"). We do not operate or control in any respect any information, products, or services on such Third-Party Sites linked to by us via the QR Codes included in this publication, and we assume no responsibility for any materials you may access using the QR Codes. Your use of the QR Codes may be subject to terms, limitations, or restrictions set forth in the applicable terms of use or otherwise established by the owners of the Third-Party Sites. Our linking to such Third-Party Sites via the QR Codes does not imply an endorsement or sponsorship of such Third-Party Sites, or the information, products, or services offered on or through the Third-Party Sites, nor does it imply an endorsement or sponsorship of this publication by the owners of such Third-Party Sites.

CONTENTS

KEY ICONS TO LOOK FOR

 Educational Videos: Readers can view videos by scanning our QR codes, providing them with additional educational content to supplement the text. Examples include news coverage, moments in history, speeches, iconic moments, and much more!

 Series Glossary of Key Terms: This back-of-the-book glossary contains terminology used throughout this series. Words found here increase the reader's ability to read and comprehend higher-level books and articles in this field.

 Research Projects: Readers are pointed toward areas of further inquiry connected to each chapter. Suggestions are provided for projects that encourage deeper research and analysis.

INTRODUCTION

There was an odd phenomenon in America in the 1950s that motorists of a lesser sort, say those driving Detroit iron, probably missed.

Every once in a while a split- or oval-window Volkswagen Beetle would be traveling down a road when it encountered a similar bug being driven in the opposite direction. The drivers would flash their lights almost simultaneously or shoot an arm out the window and flash the victory sign. The more subtle driver might give a palms-up wave without his hand leaving the steering wheel.

It was silent acknowledgment that these two drivers shared something special. This is perhaps commonplace today, when someone driving, say, a thirty-year-old car sees an identical one coming up alongside; but in the fifties, when sameness was all but revered—with numerous men dressing in the same gray flannel suits and driving Chevrolet Bel-Airs and Ford Fairlanes—it was almost subversive.

Postwar America was flush with wealth. The car-buying public had been deprived of new cars for nearly four years and they hungered for anything new. It was a seller's market. In the years immediately after the war, waiting lists for new cars were long and prices were high. Anything sold. Studebaker, long the perennial underdog in automotive sales, was having banner years in sales. President Dwight D. Eisenhower's administration was friendly to business, particularly the automotive industry. Production was high, labor strife was minimal, and people had disposable income.

Detroit responded to these boom years with big cars bedecked with lots of chrome. It reflected the country's position in the world: fat and happy. Engineering took a back seat to design. Harley Earl, the design chief for General Motors, took his styling cue from jet aircraft and, later, spacecraft. Chrysler's design guru, Virgil Exner, focused his energies on

This 1966 bug sports a new 1300 engine that offered 50 horsepower and bragging rights for Volkswagen by placing "1300" on the rear decklid.

The panel van, which was sometimes decorated by owners with psychedelic images, was a popular seller. This is the 1964 model.

aerodynamic styling and planted fins on his cars. This began a fin frenzy during the second half of the 1950s that reached its pinnacle with the Earl's '59 Cadillac. These rolling behemoths were heavy, guzzled gallons of gasoline, and were one pain in the neck to park and maintain. Brakes were subpar and handling was sluggish.

Yet there was not much of a hue and cry for anything different. The Harley Earls of Detroit decided what the public should drive and there wasn't much point in debating the issue.

Volkswagen's American debut in 1949 certainly didn't change matters. After all, General Motors toyed with the idea of building a small, economical car with its Cadet. But it rejected the plan because it was not cost effective. VW sold just two Beetles in '49, so there weren't a whole lot of folks beating down dealers' doors for an alternative to Detroit's offerings. The bug then was an anomaly in a sea of whales on the American roadway.

Rather, Volkswagen began selling cars in the United States for different reasons. Yes, it was economical, with horsepower from its four-cylinder rear-mounted air-cooled engine ranging from 25 to 30. It got twenty-plus miles to the gallon; a Buick Roadmaster was lucky to get ten. And it was quick and nimble. But then that could be had in a much more stylish import like Jaguar, MG, or Triumph.

What set the Volkswagen apart from the rest of the field was its homely looks. Its rounded fenders, running boards, and rear split window gave it a prewar look. It certainly could not be called pretty by postwar U.S. standards. But this was the very thing that attracted buyers. The Volkswagen soon became a symbol of the intellectual elite. College professors and graduate students started driving them around town. Beat generation bohemians saw it as a vehicle that allowed them to thumb their noses at the complacent largess of American society.

By 1957 there were more than two hundred thousand VWs on the road. It was becoming less of a novelty and more of a practical means to get around. A year later a severe recession hit and labor strikes in the steel industry put a crimp in automotive production. The Soviet Union had beaten the United States in the space race and suddenly the good life was beginning to change. Still, American cars remained the same. The 1958 Buick Limited typified General Motors' philosophy that bigger was better. As long as there was more horsepower under the hood and more chrome plastered on the outside, what could go wrong?

The problem was that the buying public was beginning to weary of the onslaught of such excess. Cleaner, more lithe lines in design were sought. Quicker handling, better braking ability, and the luxury of driving a car to the market and back without a stop at the gas station became more and more desirable.

Volkswagen had been in America for ten years before American automakers saw the need for a light, economical compact car. General Motors, Ford, and Chrysler also began to view Volkswagen as a threat as VW sales continued to climb at a steady rate. U.S. Beetle sales leaped from a modest 33,662 in 1955 to 84,677 in 1959 and 112,027 in 1960. The Microbus—an odd duck from the moment it hit U.S. roads in 1950 with two sales—saw total production rise from 49,907 (3,189 sales in the U.S.) in 1955 to 121,453 (32,423 sales in the U.S.) in 1959.

Detroit would soon enough get the message that change was needed.

Rambler had been making small cars for years, but sales had always been mediocre. Studebaker was first out of the gate with a new compact car, the Lark, in 1959. Ford followed with its Falcon in 1960, along with Chevrolet's Corvair and Plymouth's Valiant. Unfortunately for Detroit, however, the horse was already out of the barn door, and Volkswagen would survive them all as sales continued to skyrocket.

What was the driving force behind the plain-Jane Beetle? Mid-sixties Falcons and the Corvair were certainly more sporty and offered many more options than the bug. Marketing played a huge part in winning the confidence of American buyers. Volkswagen knew its bug was ugly, yet instead of tinkering with its design the company exploited its looks with self-deprecating advertisements. What could be more appropriate than having actor Dustin Hoffman, in the early sixties, hawking the Volkswagen?

Still, while Volkswagen was telling its buyers that beauty was in the eye of the beholder, it gave them alternatives, just in case the buyer didn't think that good looks were not as subjective as Volkswagen had suggested.

VW came up with not only the Microbus but the Karmann Ghia (its design, oddly enough, executed by Chrysler's Virgil Exner) and the Type III Notchback, Squareback, and Fastback models.

By the end of the sixties Corvair was gone. The Valiant and the Falcon soon followed. The Beetle had nearly another decade to go in the United States, though production in Mexico continues to this day.

Volkswagen saw the future and seized it. Detroit saw the future and wanted to cling to the past. VW continues to be a leader in automaking, but is no longer king. Yet it opened the door for Japanese imports and forced U.S. automakers to reexamine their product. It took the oil crisis and subsequent gasoline shortages in 1973 to wake Detroit up and fully embrace the compact car, but it was the specter of Volkswagen at its heels that changed the face of the American automobile.

FOLLOWING PAGE: The 1996 GTI came with a wide variety of options including a 5-speed manual transmission or automatic transmission.

By the 1970s, the Beetle served the dreams of custom car owners, radically altering its appearance by enlarging engine capacity and lowering its stance for a racing feel.

CHAPTER ONE

THE BEETLE

It stands to reason that the Volkswagen Beetle's roots should be found in humble beginnings. Yet its history is steeped in luxury and high-performance engineering. The bug is perhaps best described as the offspring of some of the greatest feats performed by Mercedes-Benz and another rear-engine trailblazer, the Porsche.

To understand the success of the Volkswagen Beetle as well as its infamous link to Nazi Germany, one must understand the vision its makers saw as early as 1930. Simply put, it was a car that was to serve the masses.

Porsche

Ferdinand Porsche, whose name would become synonymous with wealth and full-throttle power, cut his engineering teeth working in his family's metalsmith shop as a teenager. Early in his life he displayed an aptitude for building things. He developed a full electrical system for his family home, then an electric motor—both before the turn of the century. In 1900, he developed an electric automobile.

The lure of aviation in its early days was strong. Porsche abandoned the development of electric cars in 1907 and switched to aviation engines. Perhaps his most successful project was the Austro-Daimler aviation engine. In 1912 he designed an air-cooled 90-horsepower aviation engine that served as the blueprint for the Volkswagen rear-mounted engine which would service VWs well into the 1980s.

Porsche's success with the aviation engine earned him directorship of Austro-Daimler in Stuttgart. He then turned his attention again to automobiles, developing six-cylinder models. Early in his tenure as director Porsche developed the K Series Mercedes-Benz, which attracted wide attention from the motoring public. It was a brutish 6-liter model that developed 110-horsepower at normal speeds. It could kick up to 160-horsepower when the *kompressor* was punched to engage the supercharger. The K Series was the first supercharged Mercedes-Benz and would set the stage for some of the most innovative machines to compete in auto racing.

At the dawn of the 1930s, Porsche founded his own design firm, Porsche Buro, selecting the best men from Austro-Daimler and other companies to form his team. He brought in Austro-Daimler alumnus engineer Karl Rabe and engineer Joseph Kales and designer Erwin Komenda. Also joining Porsche was his son, Ferdinand "Ferry" Porsche, Jr. Porsche's new company was named Dr.-Ing. h.c. Ferdinand Porsche GmbH.

The Prototypes

By 1931, the seeds of the Volkswagen Beetle were planted. The team designed a saloon with a streamlined body, pontoon-type fenders, fully independent suspension, and an engine mounted in the rear. It was the antithesis of the Mercedes-Benz. It was small, economical, and spartan in appointments and comfort; still, it was equally reliable to the Mercedes.

Porsche wanted a rear-engine vehicle because he sought to eliminate the long driveshaft but also to maintain a safe weight distribution. To keep the car light, he had Kales develop an air-cooled engine constructed of aluminum and magnesium castings. The early efforts resulted in a water-cooled 1.2-liter five-cylinder radial engine. The car was dubbed *Volksauto* (people's car).

The duty of actual construction was left to a motorcycle manufacturing company called Zundapp. The car was test driven in 1932. Zundapp had agreed to begin production but motorcycle demand in Germany was so high that it abandoned plans to concentrate solely on the two-wheelers.

Porsche now found himself looking for another builder. He went to NSU, which would help him create the flat-four boxer engine.

Adolf Hitler assumed power in Germany in 1933, and on January 14, 1934, Porsche submitted a proposal for a "people's car" to the new German Reich government. An agreement was signed between Porsche and the Reichsverband der Automobilindustrie (RDA), with an budget of 20,000 Reichsmark per month.

The RDA, however, didn't exactly embrace Porsche's vision of a car for the working stiff. RDA's interests were in luxury cars. As a consequence, it didn't provide much support for Porsche's new car. Hitler himself was eager to get the car produced so the RDA was put in a position to help Porsche whether RDA liked it or not. Porsche was under RDA orders to produce a car with a wheelbase of less than 100 inches and a 26-horsepower engine that could hit a top speed of 60 mph and get a minimum of 50 miles per gallon of gasoline. All this for a retail price tag of 1,500 Reichsmark for the buyer.

Hitler demanded a car that required minimal maintenance or repair, could seat four or five people, and that the engine be air-cooled. Porsche had refused to construct his

Daimler-Benz was brought in to help build the VW3 and later the VW30 prototypes. This VW30 prototype had its headlamps moved to the fenders. The distinct fastback also emerged with this model. Doors were still hinged at the rear, but the VW30's rear quarter panel windows were enlarged considerably from the VW3 prototype.

Adolf Hitler, center, behind two officers in overcoats, inspects a convertible Beetle during ceremonies in the late 1930s. Hitler demanded an aggressive campaign to supply the German people with an affordable car.

cars with the traditional use of cheap steel and wood. He went with a unibody construction with sheet metal to ensure better stability and handling.

By the end of 1934, Porsche had his car. It was powered by a 984-cc air-cooled engine that generated 22-horsepower with a 5.8-to-1 compression ratio. It was clearly the forerunner to the Beetle that would hit U.S. shores in 1949. Yet is was without many of the characteristics found on the later popular Beetles. Not included in the prototype design was the distinct split rear window (or pretzel window), running boards, or bumpers. The headlamps were mounted on the front bonnet and the doors were hinged at the rear.

Daimler-Benz was then enlisted to construct bodies for the VW3 and later the VW30 prototypes. Headlamps were moved to the fenders and the distinct fastback emerged. Doors were still hinged at the rear, but the VW30's rear quarter-panel windows were enlarged considerably from the VW3 prototype.

The prototype would undergo a series of modest changes over the next three years, including the addition of an external oil cooler to solve some cooling problems. Erwin Komenda is credited for the final design of the VW30 prototype. When the project was turned over to the Deutsche Arbeitsfront (DAF), Nazi storm troopers began to vigorously test the vehicle. Porsche, meanwhile, went to the United States to observe Detroit's automaking techniques and to find more engineers of German ancestry to help him establish an automobile factory.

Sitting on a 94.5-inch wheelbase and on 16-inch wheels, the Schwimmwagen handled well in high terrain and high water areas. In all, only 14,276 Schwimm-wagens were built. This is a rare, but pristine example of German technology during World War II.

Under British control at the end of World War II, Volkswagen Beetles began to move swiftly off the assembly line. Early Beetles used Kubelwagen *chassis.*

The Beetle Is Born

By 1938 the Series 38 had emerged, now sporting a split rear window. It was identified as the KdF-Wagen (*Kraft durch Freude,* or "Strength Through Joy"). In March, the foundation was laid for the Volkswagen factory near Fallersleben. In September a new company, Volkswagenwerk GmbH, was formed to produce the cars.

The new car was not sold on a cash basis but through a stamp-purchase plan. German workers purchased stamps each week. When the worker's stamp card was full, he could turn it in for a new Volkswagen. An estimated 170,000 stamp-purchase plan applications were filed with Volkswagen between August 1, 1938, and the end of 1939. Very few workers received their cars, however, due to the outbreak of war.

Production of the civilian Beetle was almost nonexistent. When war broke out in September 1939, production was shifted to military use. The factory began outputting the military Kubelwagen, the German equivalent to the Jeep, powered by a much stronger 1131-cc engine which generated 25-horsepower. The factory also built the amphibious Schwimmwagen.

The Kubelwagen was a ubiquitous all-purpose vehicle in Europe during the war, becoming instantly recognizable to later generations through films about World War II. Sitting on a 94.5-inch wheelbase and on 16-inch wheels, the Kubelwagen was perched high off the ground for easy and nimble handling over rough terrain—from the deserts of North African to the snow-covered expanse of the Soviet Union. These vehicles were virtually all soft-tops with four steel doors and a large fuel tank under an angular nose, with the spare tire mounted on top.

In all 50,788 Kubelwagens and 14,276 Schwimmwagens were built. Through 1945 only 630 Beetles were produced. While these numbers are paltry compared to U.S. war production of vehicles, the Kubelwagen played a vital role in the survival of Volkswagen during the tenuous days following the Allied victory in Europe in May 1945.

Daytime bombing raids by American aircraft destroyed two-thirds of the Volkswagen factory buildings in 1944, killing 73 and injuring 160 workers. When the war ended the plant fell into British hands. This was fortuitous for the Germans, however. The American military had no interest in the plant, and it therefore surely would have suffered from neglect; and the Russians inevitably would have cannibalized what was left.

The British military had plans for the plant. The English were less interested in building cars than they were returning the German population to a normal way of life. British Major Ivan Hirst was put in charge of rebuilding the German morale and making residents productive again. British, American, and Australian automakers were not interested in the Volkswagen and offered little help in rebuilding the plant. Henry Ford II, in fact, saw absolutely no future in the Volkswagen. It was left to Hirst to find a way to bring the Volkswagen back to life. Ferdinand Porsche was long out of the picture by this time, remaining in French custody to help develop the Renault 4CV as a German prisoner of war from V-E Day until 1947. When he was released, he joined his son, Ferry, to help develop the Porsche 356 sports car in Germany.

The 1,000th Beetle moves off the assembly line in March 1946. The British military still supervised production and management of the factory. Production of the little car far exceeded early expectations.

The Beetle's Rise from the Ashes

In May 1945, just three weeks after Germany's surrender to the Allies, Major Hirst called a town meeting to establish a "Volkswagen town." The new name for the town was "Wolfsburg"—a name taken from a nearby castle—and the factory would be reopened as the Wolfsburg Motor Works. By the end of the year, 1,785 vehicles, mostly Kubelwagens, were built. An order was placed by the British military for twenty thousand civilian Volkswagens. These vehicles were saloons and built primarily from Kubelwagen chassis, hence the high ground clearance on these early models. Within a year, ten thousand Volkswagen Beetles were produced, with most going to British military forces or various branches of the new German government. No Beetles, though, were available to the public.

In 1947 Heinrich (Heinz) Nordhoff was named managing director of the Volkswagen factory. He immediately established a plan for international distribution of the car. He also viewed factory workers as partners rather than merely employees—a practice employed by Volkswagen to this day—and as a consequence production reached high levels. By 1948 twenty-five thousand Volkswagens had been built since the war ended. Two years after Nordhoff assumed the directorship, the British relinquished control of the operation. Volkswagen production was returned at last to German control.

This 1949 Volkswagen Beetle displays features not found on early postwar production models with chrome trim, chrome bumpers and chrome hubcaps. Only two Beetles were sold in the United States for the 1949 model year.

Design modifications for the 1949–52 Beetle were few, although chrome was more heavily used. The famous "Wolfsburg" badge made an appearance, as evident on this 1950 model. By March 1950, 100,000 VWs had been produced, but only 328 saw American shores for the 1950 model year.

Another VW that achieved workhorse status is this 1963 pickup, which did not gain much popularity in the United States when new, and is now considered a much desired collector's item among enthusiasts today.

The 1946–48 Beetle is a study in minimalism. Its wheelbase was 94.5 inches with an overall length of 160 inches. Horsepower started with 24 then grew to 30 by the end of the decade. The four-speed gearbox was unsynchronized, which meant drivers had to double-clutch to change gears. And it featured the now famous split rear window.

The most striking feature about these early versions is the virtual absence of any chrome. Bumpers and even hubcaps were painted the color of the body. Chrome trim on the windows and doors was absent. It also featured items long since dead on American-made cars. It contained a notch below the rear bumper for a hand crank as well as running boards. Semaphores were located on the B-pillars as turn indicators. The "Pope's Nose" rear stop lamp and license plate light house remained until 1952. In addition, the gas tank was located under the front hood, which meant the driver had to raise the hood every time he or she wanted to fill up. On the dashboard were a pair of open glove compartments—cubby holes, if you will. The only instrument was a speedometer. No gas gauge was available until 1962, but a lever underneath the dash could be flipped to activate a one-gallon reserve gas tank for use when the car was about to run out of fuel.

In all, 9,931 VWs were produced in 1946; 8,940 in '47; and 19,127 in '48. Not one was for U.S. export.

Production leaped to 46,646 in 1949, but only two Beetles were exported to the United States. One model was displayed at the German Industrial Exhibition in New York, but public acceptance was virtually nonexistent. Dutch importer Ben Pon had attempted to interest Americans in the car with

Another collector's item is this 18-window microbus with a fabric sunroof. Many of these transporters were lowered and painted in elaborate two-tone schemes by West Coast collectors.

little success. And Max Hoffman, whose New York company was the premier importer of European cars, had little interest in Volkswagen. It was Hoffman who would demand in the early 1950s that Porsche send its 356 roadsters with a larger engine displacement because he believed the sports car was too underpowered for American tastes. Volkswagen exports to other European countries, however, were in full swing. Denmark, Luxembourg, Sweden, Belgium, and Switzerland accounted for almost a quarter of all VW sales.

By March 1950 a hundred thousand VWs had been produced, though only 328 saw American shores for the 1950 model year.

Production also began at this time for the cabriolet convertible (built by the Karmann coachbuilding firm in Osnabruck) and the Transporter. The Transporter soon began a steady climb in popularity that would emulate the sales of the Beetle. During its first months of existence, about sixty Transporters were produced daily. Between 1949 and 1967, VW Transporters included the panelvan, Kombi, Microbus, the single and crewcab pickups, and the ambulance. The Westphalia camper became popular in the 1960s and endured in two subsequent generations through the 1980s.

The split rear window and "Pope's Nose" license plate lamp makes this 1950 car a desirable model for collectors. Sales steadily climbed in Europe but were modest at best in the United States.

The 1964 panel van offers a partition between the cab and cargo area. Note the inset for the spare tire and the air vents at the top-right quarter panels for ventilation.

The 1965 Volkswagen bus offered a 1500-cc engine, enough power to handle modest loads.

The 1963 Kombi bus is a no-non-sense workhorse with few luxuries. Note this stripped down version. It is equipped with painted bumpers and hubcaps, no rear bench and no sound-deadening carpet. A passenger rearview mirror also is absent.

Three generations of Type II Volks-wagens. Production of the first genera-tion at top left began in 1950, the second generation at top right is the 1968 model, and the Vanagon began production in 1979.

The pop top gives occupants standing room to take in the view and observe their surroundings, as shown in this VW promotional photograph.

FOLLOWING PAGE: The third generation campers didn't quite match the popularity of the first and second generation models, but still offered comfort and economy.

Second generation campers achieved much popularity during the 1970s, especially with young families. Here is a 1978 model with pop top that could comfortably sleep four people.

The rear view of a 1979 Vanagon.

Simple and functional, the 1953 Beetle appealed to many motorists who were interested in economy. The 1131-cc engine served that purpose by achieving 34 miles per gallon.

Design modifications were made for the 1949–52 Beetles, but what changes were made gave the car a more appealing look. Chrome finally made an appearance. The bumpers and hubcaps were now chrome; the beltline, running boards, and hood also were trimmed in chrome. Perhaps the most noticeable difference in the 1952 model was the addition of vent flaps to the front quarter panels on export models. The vents would be dropped the following model year when VW recognized that window vents were more practical. The attractive "Wolfsburg" badge on the front hood also appeared at this point and would remain until 1962. The engine remained virtually the same as previous years with a 1131-cc engine that could hit a top speed of 65 mph and get about 34 miles per gallon. Hydraulic brakes replaced the outdated mechanical version.

For 1953 the split rear window was dropped in favor of the oval version, and would remain through 1957 models. This allowed for 23 percent more visibility and was the most significant change in the appearance of the bug since 1946. The transmission now had three synchronized gears, replacing the old crashbox.

Production stalled somewhat for 1952, with the Korean War limiting steel production.

Beetle history

But by 1953, 151,323 Beetles were produced, with 1,139 exported to the United States. Production for 1954 U.S. export sales, however, leaped to 8,086. In 1955 U.S. exports numbered 33,662, setting in motion a meteoric climb through the fifties that would see American automakers scrambling to come up with their own compact car models for the 1959 and 1960 model years. Exports worldwide went to eighty-six countries. In Germany, Volkswagen produced 42.5 percent of all its cars and 40 percent of all light commercial vehicles.

More power was available for 1954 with the engine displacement increased to 1192 cc to generate 36-horsepower with a compression ratio of 6.6-to-l. The engine featured larger intake valves. The cylinder heads were redesigned to provide better cooling for the valves and plugs. The "1200" engine would see service through the 1965 model year and proved to be the most economical and reliable of any version. Power for the 1200 would be boosted in 1961 to 40-horsepower with a 7-to-l compression ratio.

Significant improvements would follow with the 1955 model year. Semaphores on the B-pillars were removed and replaced with nipple-shaped turn indicator lights on the front fenders. The top window of the taillamp was eliminated and a dished steering wheel was added. Complementing the changes was the addition of the Karmann Ghia coupe to the Volkswagen line, a new advertising blitz directed at American buyers with about $100 knocked off the retail price for U.S. imports.

The Karmann Ghia was actually produced for the 1956 model year, but the new Ghias were ready as early as August 1955. Its introduction helped Volkswagen achieve its most successful year. Total production climbed by nearly ninety thousand units over the previous year. About six thousand employees were added to the payroll, with a total of 970 German dealerships and 2,498 abroad.

Volkswagen continued to make minor changes with each model year. While it didn't intend to change the basic shape of the Beetle, it recognized that its look was dated. Some of the more significant changes occurred in 1958, with a larger rear window replacing the oval window, a larger windshield, and front turn indicators moved from the bottom of the front fenders to the top. In 1961 larger taillamps replaced the wholly inadequate smaller versions. Alone, these changes were not going to attract wild enthusiasm, although sales continued to climb at a very satisfying rate.

The company was then as healthy as ever with more than fifty thousand factory workers employed by Volkswagen by the end of the fifties. Production at factories in Wolfsburg, Braunschweig, and Hanover were humming along at full capacity, with a lengthy back-order list continuing to grow. To accommodate the increasing demand, Volkswagen purchased property in Kassel in October 1957. And on December 28, 1957, the two-millionth Volkswagen rolled off the assembly line at Wolfsburg. For the 1960 model year, sales in the United States alone reached more than 118,000.

Karmann Ghia and the Transporter helped sales, but to keep interest alive in its cars, VW began to explore other options. The two-door 1500 sedan or "Notchback" debuted in 1961 but wouldn't reach U.S. shores until 1966. It also would bring the Squareback and Fastback versions as well.

To keep buyers coming back to the showroom, Volkswagen developed an engine exchange program. The program had been in effect since 1948 and it allowed VW owners an opportunity to save over 50 percent on the price of a new engine. Over a ten-year period a quarter-million engines were exchanged. With the exchange owners received a completely new engine and a warranty.

Hebmuller

While the debate over the beauty of the bug is a question for the ages, few collectors and enthusiasts would deny that the Hebmuller cabriolet may be the most gorgeous Volkswagen of them all.

Notwithstanding the graceful lines of the Karmann Ghia, the Hebmuller captures a unique quality that recalls a sportiness but remains unmistakably Volkswagen.

While Karmann is commonly regarded as the coachbuilder of all Volkswagen cabriolets, Joseph Hebmuller & Sons performed building services for the roadster versions. Joseph Hebmuller founded his company in 1889 in Wuppertal, Germany. When he died in 1919, his four sons began to focus their work on body modifications. They counted Hanomag, Opel, and Ford as regular customers.

When Heinz Nordhoff began plans to build a cabriolet version of the Beetle, he selected Karmann to construct the four-seater model and Hebmuller for the two-seater version. Both coachbuilders were under orders to use the Beetle chassis and running gear and make as few modifications as possible.

Because Hebmuller was constructing a two-seater, the rear deck lid was much longer and resembled the front boot, giving it a "is it coming or going?" look. At first glance, the rear deck lid did indeed look like the front boot. Rather, it was a hand-formed panel with intake louvers for the air-cooled engine. Early prototypes featured the "Pope's Nose" license plate light, 1946/47 VW bumpers with over-riders, large VW-logo hubcaps, and large horns mounted flush into the fenders. The Pope's Nose was later replaced by a more streamlined version with a spine that started at the top of the deck lid and flared down and out, giving it a decidedly art deco appearance.

Though the Hebmuller was indeed a stunning example of styling, its makers struggled with severe flex problems. With the initial prototypes, the doors became badly misaligned after only a few miles of driving. In addition, the windscreen area would crack when the front hood was clipped into place. Hebmuller was forced to strengthen the body, much more than what Karmann had to deal with in the four-seater cabriolets.

The "Wolfsburg" badge for the 1953 Beetle. It would remain on the sedans through the 1962 model year. Wolfsburg was actually a British designation for the Volkswagen factory.

To solve the windscreen problem, a reinforced tubular frame was installed into the windscreen while a sturdy steel plate was welded into the base. The sills also were installed with a heavy box section and strengthened with additional panels. By April 1949, a rigid, strong body was in place. Two months later Volkswagen ordered two thousand Type 14A models.

Perhaps the most attractive element of the cabriolet was the fact that its top folded neatly behind the rear seat with a tonneau cover fitted over the top. Another perk to owning a Hebmuller was the generous use of leather in its seats and door panels.

Most of the early Hebmullers were painted in black, but two-tone designs soon became the car's trademark, with black the dominant color. Semaphores were mounted on the front quarter panels.

The future looked bright for the company. In June 1949, it produced twenty-seven cabriolets, then twenty-eight in July. But a fire broke out in a paint spraying booth on July 23, 1949, and spread into a portion of the production area. Four weeks later production resumed, with twenty-four cars produced in August, but only seventeen rolled off the assembly line in September. For November 104 units were produced with 119 listed for December.

Hebmuller soon began to suffer from severe financial problems, however, although it is unclear whether or not they were related to the fire. Production remained for a short period at about a hundred cars per month but fell to only seventy-seven in March 1950, then a paltry seventeen in April of that year. In August 1951 only one unit was built. By 1952, the company had filed for bankruptcy.

In May 1952 Karmann took over production, building twelve units, but producing only one more by the end of the year. And in February 1953 the last Hebmuller rolled off the Karmann line. Volkswagen records show that 696 Hebmullers were produced, although some sources say as many as 750 were manufactured.

All Hebmullers were cabriolets, although it is known that at least one 2+2 coupe was constructed, with hinged rear quarter windows and a B-pillar that sported semaphores. Its rear deck lid was more bulbous than its cabriolet cousin.

Today the Hebmuller is probably the most rare of the Volkswagen types, with around a hundred surviving examples. If Hebmuller had stayed healthy, who knows what kind of success it would have enjoyed.

The big change for the 1953 model year was the elimination of the split rear window in favor of the oval version that would remain until 1957. Note that the "Pope's Nose" license plate lamp also disappeared by this time. This is a 1953 model.

The 1967 Volkswagen, especially the convertible, has long been considered by enthusiasts as perhaps the prettiest Beetle produced before U.S. safety regulations put a stranglehold on design. It had a rounder decklid, sealed headlamps in a single unit, and slimmer chrome trim.

CHAPTER TWO

GROWTH COMES QUICKLY

Through the early- and mid-sixties, the Beetle began to shed some of the old-style features that hadn't been found on American-made cars since the 1940s. Much to the relief of die-hard VW fans, a fuel gauge was finally installed, replacing the one-gallon reserve fuel tap. The gauge was separate from the speedometer from 1962 to 1967, then combined with the speedometer from 1968 onward. Plastic taillamps replaced glass and the front hood was spring balanced. Leatherette headliner replaced cloth in 1962. Metal replaced the fabric/nylon for the sunroof in the 1964 model year.

By 1966 the "1300" engine debuted, offering 50-horsepower. For the first time, VW advertised its engine displacement on its models by placing "1300" on the rear deck lid.

The 1967 Beetle, considered by enthusiasts as perhaps the most attractive bug built before U.S. safety requirements resulted in changes to its look, is the culmination of all prior Volkswagen improvements. The first noticeable change was under the deck lid with a new 1500-cc, 53-horsepower engine (Squareback and Fastback models' pancake engines received a 1600-cc displacement). The deck lid was now squared-off, giving the Beetle a more compact look. The "1300" displayed on the deck lid of the 1966 model was replaced not with a "1500" script but instead with "Volkswagen."

The electrical system was changed by mid-year to a 12-volt system instead of the archaic 6-volt version for U.S. models. Generator capacity was increased from 180 to 360 watts. Outside door handles were now push button and the inside door handles newly recessed and made of plastic, which was being used more extensively for the first time. Headlamps were the same size as those on previous models but backup lights were mounted on the rear bumper. Headlamps, too, were now a single unit instead of the recessed nacelles mounted behind glass. Finally, chrome trim along the beltline was now slimmer.

The 1967 Beetle was truly an attractive car, and buyers responded to its modest facelift. A total of 454,801 VWs—including 314,343 bugs—were sold in the United States, including tourist deliveries. Tourist deliveries had surged as VW's "See Europe by Volkswagen" program became more popular.

The 1968 model saw many changes, and perhaps for purists a move away from the uniqueness of the Beetle. It was inevitable, really, as emission control and safety standards imposed by the U.S. government began to force Volkswagen to modify the look and per-formance of their cars. Still, Volkswagen fared considerably better than other imports. British sports cars, in particular, were suffering from a variety of problems, many of which were quality control and management issues exacerbated by U.S. government regulation. MG, Jensen, and Austin-Healy, among other European automakers, were seeing sales dwindle as it became increasingly difficult to export cars to the United States.

The model year 1964 saw modest, but significant changes in the Beetle with a larger license plate lamp, a roomier interior, and a slight increase in power output.

The 1966 Beetle typified the counter-culture's desire for economical but unusual transportation, making it a symbol of the anti-establishment.

Still Volkswagen continued to have banner years in U.S. sales. In 1968, 582,009 VWs were sold, including more than 400,000 bugs. But it was slowly changing into a different car.

Single bar bumpers with a single black stripe now appeared as well as larger rear taillamps with integrated backup lights. The gas filler was now located externally on the right front quarter panel. Headrests were integrated into front seats, giving a bulkier appearance and the illusion of less roominess. These models also had an automatic stick shift option that allowed the driver to shift gears without using a clutch. It was somewhat cumbersome and not thought to be reliable. In all, 1.9 million Volkswagens were produced worldwide for that model year.

With the 1970s, VW began to turn away from rear-mounted air-cooled engines and the standard Beetle. Its Type 411, a more traditional-looking sedan, debuted in 1969 and became available for the American market in 1973. Also appealing that year was the Type 181 Thing, which resembled the World War II–era Kubelwagen. One reason for the changes were the acquisitions of both Audi and NSU, which allowed VW to begin production of front-mounted engines. Other traditional-looking sedans were the Dasher, debuting in 1974, and the Rabbit, appearing in 1975.

The model year 1973 saw the Volkswagen Beetle surpass the Ford Model T in total production. Along with the model year came the Super Beetle, the most drastic change to the body style ever. The most visible changes were the curved windshield, huge round taillamps, and McPherson struts which lengthened the front end by 4 inches. The standard Beetle was still available with its flat windshield and its 94.5-inch wheelbase.

Actors Dean Jones and Michele Lee are whisked under a row of saluting bugs from the 1969 film The Love Bug. *The film sparked sales and fueled America's fascination with the little critter.*

These snow-covered bugs in an eastern American town appear to be 1969 models.

The Beetle's days were dwindling as sales had dropped steadily since its peak year in 1968. More models were introduced into the line but sales continued to decline. And sales for the 1974 model year fell alarmingly to only 226,098 in the United States, with a lion's share of the blame going to the 1973 oil crisis in which buyers put off buying new cars.

By 1977, the last year the Volkswagen Beetle was shipped to the U.S., only 12,090 units were sold. On January 10, 1980, the last Beetle convertible rolled off the Karmann assembly line in Osnabruck. In all, 330,281 convertibles had been built there.

Karmann and Ghia

Volkswagen in the mid-1950s was determined to focus its attention on a single body style. Production was leaping ahead as demands for exports to the United States, South Africa, and Germany's European neighbors grew. Its workforce was increasing annually by the hundreds.

Even so, Volkswagen acknowledged that to remain competitive in the bountiful postwar years with old stalwarts like Ford, General Motors, and Chrysler, it needed to bolster its image. European car makers in particular produced bland, underpowered, but functional cars. To tap into the American market, especially among single men and women who earned good wages and had disposable income, Volkswagen sought a car that would bring such buyers into the showroom.

Baja Bugs have been around since the mid and late 1960s, but customizers have gone the extra mile with some pretty clean designs. Usually the nose and rear are chopped with a reinforced rear steel guard to protect the open engine. This is a 1970 convertible.

The sedan version of the Karmann Ghia, originally designed by Virgil Exner for Chrysler. When Chrysler rejected the car as too European and too sporty for its line, the design was left to Ghia coach-builders of Italy. The car was transformed into a Volkswagen, but to the delight of Exner.

Exner's Original Design

Chevrolet had introduced its Corvette in 1953; Ford its Thunderbird in 1955. Chrysler, however, didn't have a sportier two-seater for its buyers. It should have. After all, this was the only Detroit automaker that had a long history of building concept cars that moved under their own power. Chrysler was the only automaker that was not reluctant to use European styling, especially Italian automobile designs, on its cars.

Enter Virgil Exner and his influence on Volkswagen design. Rather, it is probably more accurate to say that Exner was influenced by the Italians and that Exner used this influence to give Volkswagen its new image. In a round-about way the Italians executed Exner's now-famous design, and Volkswagen got its hands on it simply because Chrysler didn't have the courage to produce the car itself.

Exner's reputation as an automotive designer was forged with his signature fins on Chrysler cars. The Plymouth Fury, the Chrysler New Yorker, and the Dodge Royal Lancer were products of Exner's vivid imagination and an insistence that fins were a functional element to road handling. General Motors would follow with GM designer Harley Earl, taking the finned look to greater heights and culminating with the outlandish 1959 Cadillac Eldorado.

Virgil Exner began his automotive design career in 1934 under the tutelage of Harley Earl for GM's Art & Colour Section. He later went to work for Raymond Loewy, who had a contract with Studebaker to design cars. After World War II Exner was largely responsible for the 1947 Studebaker Champion. The Champion was the first postwar car produced that had an all-new design. Up until then Detroit automakers were still using prewar designs. The Champion had a full-envelope body, a sculptured design, and a wraparound rear window.

In 1949 Exner left Studebaker for the Chrysler Corporation. There he performed his finest design work. In the early- and mid-fifties, Exner focused a great deal of his attention on advanced styling, which would lead to Chrysler's famed idea cars. In 1950 he developed a relationship with Luigi Segre, head of Carrozzeria Ghia Coachbuilding in Turin, Italy. Segre was eager to solicit business and rebuild his company after its plant and operations were badly damaged during the war.

Exner had always been a fan of Italian automotive design. He admired the Italians' thoroughly modern approach to design with its emphasis on streamlined and slim cars. It was the sculptured look of the Italian automobile that influenced the way Exner designed Chrysler's products.

The Chrysler man would design a number of cars that were given to Ghia Coachbuilding for construction as dream cars. These concept cars were usually single prototypes, which Chrysler tested for possible mass production. None was fully realized as a mass production car, but many design elements eventually found their way onto Chrysler cars. The exception would be Exner's 1953 Chrysler Sports Coupe D'elegance, which would later emerge under the Volkswagen badge.

The D'elegance (a departure, of course, from the proper "d'Elegance") was designed by Exner in the basement of his Michigan home and constructed at the Ghia plant. It was placed on a 115-inch wheelbase and powered by a 331.1-cubic inch V-8. It featured a faux spare tire placement on the rear deck, backup lights, gunsight taillamps, and dual exhausts. It was a tour de force in styling. Clean, lithe, with a delicate roof line. However, the car would never come to be as a Chrysler and was destined to become another single knock-off prototype.

Meanwhile, Wilhelm Karmann, Jr., whose coachbuilding firm in Osnabruck, Germany built cabriolet bodies for Volkswagen, began lobbying Volkswagen for a sporty VW model. Karmann had picked up the campaign that had been led by his father, Dr. Wilhelm Karmann Sr., who had hoped to entice Volkswagen into joining the European trend of offering a sports car. The senior Karmann died in 1951 before he could interest Wolfsburg in the plan. His son continued discussions with Heinz Nordhoff that would go on at least two more years

Enter Karmann

Karmann GmbH was Germany's most distinguished coachbuilder. It was founded in 1874, and built its first automobile in 1902 for Durkopp. Just a year later it decided to specialize in coachbuilding. Karmann would maintain a profitable business, but the German depression during the 1920s put a lot of Karmann's clients out of business. Although the worldwide depression a decade later did not help matters, Karmann managed to have about six hundred workers on the payroll. World War II intervened, and during Allied bombing the Karmann plant was heavily damaged.

After the war, the Karmann operation was reduced to building wheelbarrows and other small items. It could repair automobiles but was prohibited by Allied occupational forces to build them. After much labored negotiations, Karmann was finally permitted to purchase a chassis and build a cabriolet prototype for Volkswagen. Karmann's relationship with VW from that point was cemented.

Wilhelm Karmann's idea for the design of the sports car, however, did not appeal to Nordhoff. Karmann then when to Segre, who obtained possession of Exner's design after it became apparent that Chrysler was not interested in the D'elegance. The relationship between the two men resulted in the car that would become the Karmann Ghia.

The final design eliminated the D' elegance's gunsight taillamps and faux spare tire molding on the rear deck. A rounded nose replaced the traditional grille. The bumpers were redesigned and the headlamps were slightly relocated. It was shrunk down proportionately for the Beetle 94.5-inch wheelbase, but its bug floorpan was widened by 4 inches to strengthen its side members. A front anti-roll bar was added; the steering column was angled slightly; the gear lever was shortened; and the engine was fitted with a Transporter air-filter to accommodate the low profile of the deck lid. Otherwise it was virtually the same car Exner had designed for Chrysler. Europeans were chagrined that the new Volkswagen was American-designed, but few realized its styling roots actually were to be found in Italian automotive design.

There is some controversy within automotive press circles as to whether Exner should actually be credited with the design of the Karmann Ghia. What is certain is that Exner did design the D'elegance, and the virtually identical resemblance of the D'elegance to the Karmann Ghia—not to mention Exner's relationship to Ghia—cannot be dismissed.

Each body was virtually handmade because Karmann did not have the equipment to press the panels. One of the resulting features of building a car by hand is that every seam was filled and finished in lead, giving the body a single, seamless look. The labor-intensive work required that nearly two thirds of the Karmann factory's workforce was employed in the body shop

In 1955, when the Karmann Ghia made its debut in the United States, one model went to New York and another, painted black with a gray interior, went to Chrysler. It eventually found its way to Exner's son, Virgil Exner, Jr., who drove it as a young man for some time.

The Karmann Ghia was all Volkswagen underneath with the same rear-mounted 36-horsepower flat-four engine. It had a lower center of gravity and better aerodynamics than the Beetle and consequently handled better. The rear seat was a tiny bench, but folded down for extra cargo room. The interior appointments were decidedly Volkswagen, with little flair, but there actually was a dashboard on which something could be placed. It had a round speedometer and matching-sized clock. There was no fuel gauge, of course, on the early models but it had the reserve tank lever for the extra gallon of gasoline. A Karmann badge was placed low on the front fenders.

There was nothing like the Karmann Ghia on the road. The closest sports car to it was the Morgan 4/4, which had a similar horsepower range but better acceleration. Rather than ignore or downplay its limited power, Volkswagen exploited it for marketing purposes. In a television commercial, a

The two-tone version of the Karmann Ghia was popular among U.S. buyers and still can be found on the road today. Note the styling has changed little between the 1970 model and this 1966 version.

Volkswagen went to Karmann for help in designing a cabriolet for its Karmann Ghia. Karmann strengthened members under each sill and installed rein-forcements around the door openings to minimize flex. This pretty cabriolet is a 1970 vintage.

Karmann Ghia was shown racing toward a large sheet of white paper with the intent to rip through it. Instead, it just bounced off the paper without so much as a single tear. And in magazine and newspaper advertising the Ghia was often displayed with Maseratis and Lamborghinis with the hint that at least the buyer could afford the Volkswagen.

The first Karmann Ghia rolled off the Karmann assembly line in early August 1955 for the 1956 model year. More than ten thousand units were sold the first year; 2,452 models were exported to the United States. Nearly twice that number was exported to America in 1957. When the cabriolet was introduced in 1958, overall sales for both the coupe and cabriolet leaped to eighteen thousand. Of that number, 4,700 coupes and 1,325 convertibles were exported to the United States. The added bonus of owning a cabriolet was that it always was equipped with a fuel gauge.

Horsepower was boosted to 40 in 1961. Engine displacement was enlarged to 1300 cc to generate 50-horsepower in 1965, then to 1500 cc and 53-horsepower in 1967. Disc brakes were added in 1965, and the automatic transmission—like that on the Beetle—was offered in '68. That same model year also saw the gas filler cap moved externally so the front hood did not have to be opened in order to fuel the car.

Body styling remained virtually unchanged for Karmann Ghia's nineteen-year existence. The number of U.S. exports climbed steadily over the years, peaking in 1970 at 22,952 for coupes and 5,873 for convertibles.

After the 1974 model year, the Karmann Ghia was discontinued to make way for the new Scirocco. The Kharmann Ghia had served its purpose as a sporty alternative to the Beetle, but as Volkswagen looked forward to developing water-cooled front engine models, there was no room for the Ghia.

The success of the Karmann Ghia cannot be denied. It attracted the singles market—both male and female—and spawned many custom models that survive today.

FOLLOWING PAGE: Perhaps the most dramatic changes to the bug occurred with the 1968 model year as the U.S. government imposed strict safety regulations. This 1970 model has headrests and rein-forced bumpers.

Karmann Ghia

The "Razor Edge" Karmann Ghia

Rarely seen in the United States was another Karmann Ghia effort by Volkswagen. The Type 34 Karmann Ghia—or "razor edge Ghia," as the British called it—began as a successor to the Beetle in the late fifties. Volkswagen was afraid that the market for the Beetle would become stagnant because of its elated looks. The Type 34, they believed, would upgrade the Volkswagen line.

In 1958–59 Ghia designers started shaping a new style, with Karmann to perform construction. Considered a mid-market car, the engine layout allowed for the relocation of the fan shroud so that the fan could run off the crankshaft. This allowed for room in the rear of the car as additional luggage space. Complementing the line, now identified as the Series 1500, would be Type III Volkswagens—the sedan (Notchback), station wagon (Variant or Squareback), and, later, the Fastback.

In September 1961, the entire line of the Series 1500 debuted at the Frankfurt Auto Show with the Type 34 Karmann Ghia featured as the flagship of Series 1500.

Styling for the Type 34 generated a love/hate relationship with the motoring public. Its roofline was considered awkward but its lines from the nose sweeping back along the fenders to the doors were elegant. It also featured built-in fog lamps and electric steel-sliding sunroof, rare standard equipment for such a car.

The 1962 models had a rectangular nose badge and small Karmann badges located low on the rear quarter panels. The Karmann badges were removed the following year and the round VW badge replaced the rectangular version. Disc brakes and a 1600-cc engine debuted in 1966.

Despite its focus on the mid-market crowd, the Type 34 was expensive, rivaling the cost of the Porsche 356 roadster. It was never marketed in the United States, although somehow three hundred or so made it there. Only 30 percent of the total production was exported to other countries, with England, Canada, and Australia receiving most of the cars. Mass production began in March 1962 and ended in July 1969 with 42,510 coupes completed.

The buyer never embraced the Type 34 as it went toe-to-toe with the likes of Austin-Healy and MG, which offered water-cooled engines superior to the VW's air-cooled models.

The Cabriolet

Heinz Nordhoff probably would not have been interested in the Karmann Ghia if Karmann had not made such a stunning success out of the Volkswagen cabriolet. Volkswagen had always been reluctant to give up a rolling chassis to allow a coachbuilder to work its magic on a new design. Volkswagen wanted control over such projects and its standards were incredibly high.

When building the cabriolet for Volkswagen, Karmann was faced with a simple but universal problem of convertible design—flexing. Whenever the roof is cut off a body, the chassis will suffer from severe flex. It would be a major problem for Karmann in the early 1960s when it attempted to build a convertible Type 34 ("1500") Karmann Ghia, only to be forced to abandon its plans when flex problems with this model could not be conquered.

For the cabriolet Beetle, Karmann strengthened members under each sill and provided reinforcement around the door openings. The front quarter panels were redesigned to add strength. By mid-1949, three prototypes were built, which eventually led to twenty-five pre-production models manufactured for a grueling test program. The testing proved that Karmann had beat the flexing problems. In late

August 1949, production was ordered for two thousand units. By April 1950, a thousand convertibles had been built.

Virtually all components for the cabriolet were identical to the sedan. There were, however, some minor variations. The rear louvers, placed below the rear window and above the deck lid on the sedan, were moved on the convertible to make room for the top to fold down. They were placed on the convertible's deck lid. Early models featured vertical louvers while later models featured horizontal ones. Semaphores were placed on the rear quarter panels due to the absence of a B-pillar. Perhaps the best characteristic of the cabriolet, though, was its glass (instead of plastic) rear window. It added a classiness not found on such economical and relatively spartan cars as the Volkswagen.

Reflectors, two-tone rear tail lamps, and an air intake grille on the decklid are significant changes at the dawn of the 1970s.

*This remote controlled, futuristic concept car
caused a sensation when it was shown in 1991.
Guided from a distance like a child's toy, it
could be started, moved forward, and even
parked with no one inside.*

CHAPTER THREE

MOVING FORWARD

With the dawn of the 1960s, Volkswagen's position in the automotive industry was secure. In June 1960, Volkswagenwerk GmbH became a limited company, with 60 percent of its shares now available to the public while the German government and the Lower Saxony retained 20 percent of its shares.

In September of that year, the automaker opened its French plant in Neuilly. By then half a million VWs had been exported to the United States and its ten-thousandth car rolled off the assembly line at Volkswagen do Brasil. By January 1961 Sweden had become the top European export market for VW.

While Beetle exports to the United States exceeded all the hopes and dreams of VW management, competition in Europe was beginning to stiffen. Larger, more luxurious American imports were grabbing a share of the auto market. The time was ripe to expand the line beyond the Beetle, Transporter, and Karmann Ghia.

Notchback, Squareback, Fastback

In the late fifties, a portion of the Wolfsburg factory was damaged due to a fire. The blaze was limited to a single but large building. While repairs were under way, the windows were boarded up. When the damage was repaired, the windows remained boarded to keep secret the construction of a number of prototypes for a new line. These new cars were dubbed the Type III.

When the 1960 Geneva Auto Show opened, VW maintained that no new models were being designed. However, *Sports Car Illustrated* as early as August 1959 reported that VW was indeed contemplating a new line of cars that were similar to the Austin A-40. Still, it would be nearly two years—early 1961—until Volkswagen released a photograph of the new car.

The Type III, or 1500 Sedan—also called the Notchback—debuted in 1961. It wouldn't be marketed in America, but several found their way here. Its outer appearance was radically different from the Beetle and the Karmann Ghia, but still the same old VW inside. The 1500 Variant debuted in early 1962. When the 1500 Variant was marketed in the United States, VW didn't want it confused with the Plymouth Valiant. They could not call it a station wagon because the Type II Transporters were identified by VW as a station wagon. Rather, VW identified the Variant as the Squareback for the U.S. market. The Fastback would follow in short order.

When the Squareback and Fastback were exported to the United States in late 1965 for the 1966 model year, they sported 1585 cc engines with a 7.7-to-1 compression ratio to generate 65-horsepower. These engines were significantly larger than the Beetle engines, which remained 1285 cc for the 1966 model year. While the displacement was larger, the cooling fan was mounted at the rear end of the crankshaft pulley, with the oil cooler placed

In an attempt to address environmental concerns, Volkswagen initiated a program to use some Golfs to be powered by electricity. This vehicle was produced by Stromer.

The wave of the future? Both Volvo and Toyota have introduced bi-fuel models similar to VW's Stromer experiment.

horizontally and the generator sitting low against the crankcase. This made the engine about 15 inches tall, allowing for additional cargo area above the engine. The larger engine displacement for the Squareback and Fastback accommodated the increased weight. The Squareback weighed 2,029 pounds and the Fastback 1,962 pounds, compared to the standard Beetle weighing in at 1,653 pounds. These models sat on the same 94.5-inch wheelbase as the Beetle.

Also included in the line was the Type III Karmann Ghia, but like the Notchback it never saw official U.S. export.

The 1962–63 models were virtually identical, carrying over-riders on the bumpers, chrome front turn signals, painted rear reflectors, the flat tail lamps, and high mounted side markers. They also featured a single 32PHN carburetor and knob heater control.

The basic 1964 model was stripped of a number of items. It featured no side markers, rear arm rests, pop-out windows, passenger sun visor, or over-riders. The deluxe S model, however, offered wraparound front turn indicators, chrome rear reflectors, lower side markers, larger tail lamps, chrome on the front hood lip, and dual 32PDSIT carbs. For 1965, all the Type IIIs featured the dual carbs.

When the Fastback made its debut for U.S. export in 1966, it was equipped with front disc brakes and a redesigned rearview mirror. The Type III features for the 1967 model year mirrored the same changes as those found on the Beetle, with backup lights mounted on the bumper, new heater levers and door locks, a dual master brake cylinder, and dual port heads. Mid-year saw the conversion from a 6-volt electrical system to 12 volts.

The Squareback and Fastback would remain virtually unchanged through its final model year in 1973. They enjoyed good sales and were every bit as reliable as the Beetle. As part of VW's plan to reduce its line of rear-mounted, air-cooled engines, these two models were phased out.

The Thing

While Volkswagen enjoyed success with its Type III line, it is unclear what the thinking was when it developed the VW 181 (eventually known as "The Thing"), especially for export to the United States.

The VW 181 recalled the famous Kubelwagens of World War II. The Kubelwagen (literally meaning "bucket"), Germany's answer to the American-made Jeep, was almost as versatile as that popular vehicle—a utilitarian vehicle that served a variety of purposes during the war. It was used as a small transport for men; and it could cover just about any terrain with its high ground clearance. Fitted with balloon tires it was virtually unstoppable during the North Africa campaign. A later Type 92 Kommandeurwagen appeared toward the end of the war to serve as a command vehicle for officers.

It is difficult to believe that since the Kubelwagen was so closely identified with the war, the German army, and, really, with Nazi officers, that Volkswagen management would be nostalgic for this era gone by. But then there was no denying that the Kubelwagen was a very reliable machine.

In late 1969, Volkswagen introduced for the 1970 model year the multipurpose open-air VW 181. Its primary use was as a courier vehicle by the German federal army but it soon found its way into other government services.

The Type 181 was intended as a workhorse with a modified Type 1 Karmann Ghia chassis, powered by a 44-horsepower rear-mounted air-cooled engine. It was widely used by civilians as a recreational vehicle and marketed as the Safari. Still, it looked to be a pale imitation of the Kubelwagen. The Kubelwagen's sleek angular nose was replaced by a boxed front end and its round, flowing fenders now sported square versions.

Production was transferred from the Hanover plant to Puebla, Mexico, in 1973. Late that year, Volkswagen began importing the Type 181 into the United States, where it was dubbed The Thing. A tad more than fourteen thousand Type 181s made it to America. During the first six months of 1974, nearly fifteen thousand Things were imported.

But U.S. government regulations conspired against its success. First the U.S. Department of Transportation reclassified the vehicle as a passenger

The Thing—this one a 1973 model—was an unusual, if not wacky idea by Volkswagen. An idea born from the Kubelwagen, safety and emission control regulations conspired to keep it from selling well in the United States, and it never was a popular vehicle among American buyers.

The Thing!

vehicle instead of a commercial or multipurpose unit, giving it a series of safety and emissions requirements to meet. At the same time, interest in the Type 181 lagged due to its unusual looks and confusion over whether the vehicle was designed for pleasure or for work. By late 1974 and early 1975, there were still a number of unsold Things on dealer lots.

The Thing was a noble experiment that saw success in Europe but never quite caught on in the United States. By the mid-seventies it had already faded from sight.

The New Beetle

The Beetle had become an American icon, even more so than in its home country. Americans had enjoyed a love/hate relationship with the little critter for more than thirty years. But for anyone who owned more than one VW, it was certainly a loving relationship.

In the seventies and well into the eighties, college and high school students modified their bugs, Karmann Ghias, and Transporters by lowering them, and enlarging displacement to add horsepower, to give it a throaty, powerful performance and sporty appearance. Clubs sprang up around the country and a cottage industry of accessories and custom-car parts shops sprang up. The mystique of the Beetle was cemented in American automobile lore.

Its passing was lamented by the die-hard VW fan, but those high school and college kids who spent thousands of dollars to customize their bugs were now professionals with families. Tastes changed. So it is not without some

This stark red and white interior of the Futura concept car features a console that changes its color from light green to bright red if an obstacle appears on the roadway.

The gullwing doors of the Futura concept car open to give access to both rows of seats. The glass keeps 60 percent of the thermal energy of sunlight, and has headlights of new construction. The van seats four.

The 1977 Rabbit re-
placed the venerable
Beetle. This is a four-
door model. Purists
were none too pleased
that their beloved bug
was no longer imported
into the United States.
Bug manufacturing
continued in Mexico.

A step up from the
Rabbit and Golf is the
Jetta. This is a 1982
Jetta C four-door model.
In was initially intro-
duced in 1979, four
years after the Rabbit,
and started basically, as
a Rabbit with a trunk.

The 1978 Dasher was a sportier answer to the Rabbit in the late 1970s. It enjoyed brisk sales.

Despite the dismissive label that the Rabbit convertible was a "secretary's car," it emerged as perhaps one of the most popular convertibles of the 1980s. It captured a market that was all but abandoned by U.S. automakers during the decade. This is a 1982 model.

The dashboard and instrument panel of the 1981 Golf GTI.

The 1981 Volkswagen Golf GTI was Volkswagen's sequel to the Rabbit as an economical vehicle.

The 1982 Volkswagen pickup never enjoyed the popularity or cult status as did the micro-bus or single cab pick-ups from the 1960s.

A 1983 Volkswagen Golf GTI 1800 Campaign model.

The 1985 Volkswagen Golf C Diesel enjoyed healthy sales in Europe, but the diesel power never caught on with the wary U.S. motoring public. It's the Golf chassis that is used for the 1998 Beetle.

The 1985 Golf C Diesel engine gave U.S. buyers fits, but was amazingly economical both at the gas pumps and with maintenance.

FOLLOWING PAGE:
The 1984 Volkswagen Golf GTI Cabriolet didn't look much different than the Rabbit, and didn't capture the public's imagination as the Rabbit did either.

The 1987 Volkswagen Golf C. The 16-valve engine would serve the Golf well through the years. With the fourth generation Golf, engines ranged from the all-aluminum 1.4-liter to the 1.8-liter turbocharged GTI.

Modest changes in design kept the 1987 Volkswagen Golf GTI 16-valve model looking pretty much the same as its predecessors, yet kept up with its competitors in providing a sleek and well-styled appearance.

The Scirocco, when it appeared in the late 1970s, was designed to replace the Karmann Ghia. It was an exciting alternative and captured the imagination of American buyers. This is a 1987 Scirocco Scala.

The rear, three-quarter
view of the 1987 Scirocco
Scala with spoiler.

The 2-liter, 4-cylinder
gasoline-powered engine of
the 1987 Scirocco Scala.

*The 1989
Vanagon GL
changed little
from previous
third generation
models.*

*With its roof
raised, the
1989 Vanagon
Camper offered
just enough
shelter to
provide carefree
enjoyment
of the great
outdoors.*

Popular among small, young families was the Passat, which debuted in the late 1980s. This is a 1987 Passat GLS station wagon.

Over 17.6 million Golfs have been produced, thus exceeding the entire Beetle production, including Beetles still being built in Mexico.

The 16-valve 1988 Volkswagen Jetta GTI became the mainstay of Volkswagen through the 1980s and 1990s. It was VW's answer to such cars as the Toyota Camry and mid-range Nissan products.

The 1988 Volks-
wagen Polo Rang-
er hardened back
to the auto maker's
Beetle days.

Mounted sideways
in the engine com-
partment to save
space is the 1.2-liter
engine in a 1988 Polo
Ranger. The engine
had eight overhead
valves with a braking
horsepower of about
113 at 6000 rpm.

Volkswagen
maintained
basic, no-
nonsense
styling for its
line of cars,
including this
1988 Golf GTI
convertible.

Sporty, but economical in concept, the 1989 16-valve Passat GT was ahead of its American counterparts in design. VW engineers emphasized quality and safety as its most notable features.

The 1988 VW Passat GT took over in sales of the Rabbit and Golf cars.

The 1993 Passat GLX came with
a variety of options. Its basic
engine, a 1.6-liter version, would
achieve a top speed of more than
110 mph with acceleration of
0–62 mph at 12.3 seconds. In the
1998 Passat, the 1.6-liter engine
could generate 100 braking
horsepower at 5,300 rpm.

The 1993 Passat GLX wagon
provided comfort and room
for small families but still
gave the driver a sporty feel.

This 1993 Jetta III GL sat on a 97.3-inch wheelbase and weighs a little less than 3,000 pounds. Its front suspension is state-of-the-art Mac-Pherson struts with stabilizer bar, coil springs, and telescopic shock absorbers.

The 1993 VW Corrado, powered by a 1.8-liter engine, could hit 0–60 mph in 7.5 seconds and achieve a top speed of 138 mph. This engine had a 8.0:1 compression ratio and generated 158 horsepower at 5,600 rpm.

The VW GTI, this one a 1991 model, takes to an upstate New York road. The GTI became one of the automaker's most reliable and efficient cars in its line.

Tthe 1994 Volkswagen Golf Cabriolet was at least three to four years ahead of U.S. auto makers in design. This one is powered by a 1.6-liter engine.

*The 1993 Volks-
wagen Cabriolet was
gaining popularity
in the mid 1990s.*

*The 1997 Golf GL
came with a 1.8-liter
engine that gives 125
braking horsepower.
Options included
a front driver's
seat with height
adjustment, front
sports seats, and
velour upholstery.*

The 1997 Volkswagen Cabrio was equipped with a 2-liter, 4-cylinder engine and 5-speed, manual transmission for 115 braking horsepower at 5,400 rpm. It achieved 24 miles to the gallon in the city, and 31 miles to the gallon on the highway.

The 1997 Volkswagen Cabrio was a small convertible based on the Golf hatchback. It was equipped with a large rollbar that adds structural strength and safety, but didn't detract from its top-down lines.

FOLLOWING PAGE:
The 1997 Passat TDI can achieve 24 miles per gallon in the city and up to 47 miles per gallon in highway drving. Top speeds can reach 119 mph.

In 1993 Volkswagen changed the Jetta chassis to the A3, and offered a 6-cylinder engine, known as the VR6, which stands for Vee Reihenmoter, *meaning "inline-V." These engines packed a punch with their 2.8-liter version to generate 172 horsepower. This model is a 1997 Jetta GLS.*

With black lettering against a white background, the instrument gauges on this 1997 Jetta GT give the driver a sports car feel.

The 1998 Passat GLS featured front fog lamps, an optional navigation system with autocheck display, and an elaborate GAMMA radio/cassette/CD entertainment system.

Volkswagen has come a long way since its early U.S. offerings. This 1998 Passat GLS is powered by a 1.8-liter engine.

The interior and dashboard of the 1998 Volkswagen Passat GLS.

The 1998 Volkswagen GTI differed little from the 1996 model.

expectancy that Volkswagen has attempted to recapture the very same market that helped give VW its distinct personality.

In 1994, J. Mays at the VW-Audi design studio in California developed the Concept 1, the New Beetle. It actually started out as an electric car. The New Beetle made its worldwide debut at Detroit's North American International Auto in January 1998.

Based on the chassis of the new Golf—a popular low-range priced Volkswagen sedan—the New Beetle's appearance harks back to its legendary namesake, but the similarity ended there. Volkswagen was careful to point out that the New Beetle was an entirely different car with an entirely different price tag and features. Its bulbous appearance was intact, with pontoon-type fenders and a hint of the old-style running boards. Inside, in a nod to the past, the New Beetle interior offered a large assist handle above the glove box and two assist straps above the rear seats. The buyer, however, can stop there if he or she is looking for other older Beetle characteristics. It's not a retro car.

Volkswagen says the New Beetle was significantly larger than the original, but its wheel-base is only 98.9 inches, just a little more than 4 inches longer than its namesake. Its overall length is just 161.1 inches, actually just under 3 1/2 inches shorter than the original. The difference in size, rather, is that it utilizes the interior space better with 96.3 cubic feet of interior volume.

On the dashboard was a single round instrument gauge that displays the speedometer, rev counter, and temperature and fuel gauges. Another tip of the hat to the past is a standard bud vase mounted on the dash, an updated

Interior of the 1998 beetle. Note the glass vase holding a flower, similar to the offerings to customers in the early 1950s. The resemblance ends there. It's an all-new bug.

Placed on a Golf chassis and sporting a 98.9-inch wheelbase, the 1998 VW Beetle may look like the famed bug from yester-year, but there was very little of it underneath. It was powered by a 2-liter air-cooled engine that generates 115 horse-power with a base price of $15,200.

version of the bud vases found on early Beetles.

The engine is front-mounted and water-cooled. The gasoline version is a 2-liter four-cylinder engine that generates 115-horsepower at 5200 rpm and a 10-to-1 compression ratio. A diesel version has a 1.9-liter capacity with 90-horsepower. Power is transmitted through either a 5-speed manual or 4-speed automatic transmission.

To put the car into production, Volkswagen commissioned a new plant next to its Puebla factory in southern Mexico. The New Beetle signalled a return to the forefront of American car sales for Volkswagen.

The Future

Throughout the 1980s and 1990s Volkswagen had continued to produce exciting and innovative automobiles, many of which some are seen on the previous pages. The Rabbit, Jetta, Scirocco, and even a pickup joined the famous bug in the company's stable. Those along with the New Beetle gave fans an idea of what was ahead for the company. Some of those new models became big hits, especially the New Beetle. Volkswagen has long been the "people's car" and in the new millennium, it introduced new styles and models that have led to its place today at the top of the world automotive market.

Most Beetles across the United States were sold out, with orders backlogged before they hit American shores. Demand was so high that a gray market developed in which some buyers offered 50 percent markup on the base price.

In the early 2000s, the sporty Jetta became one of Volkswagen's best-selling models. The company continued to improve the line as the decade moved along.

CHAPTER FOUR

THE WHEELS KEEP TURNING

In 2016, the Volkswagen Group became the world's No. 1 automaker surpassing Toyota. It was a major coup for Volkswagen, which owed much of its success to Golf, the company's best-selling vehicle of all time. Take that, Beetle.

When the fourth-generation Golf was introduced in 1999, it was smoother and more stylish than the preceding generations. It was even slightly longer and had a larger wheelbase, along with more interior room. By 2002, the Golf surpassed the Beetle as the most produced car in VW history. Four years later, the company introduced an updated fifth-generation compete with a five-cylinder, 2.5-liter engine with a wheelbase stretching to 101.5 inches.

For performance geeks, the Golf's steering became extremely responsive. For those who spent a lot of time driving, its interior was comfortable. Only available as a four-door hatch back, the Golf came with a standard 6.5-inch touchscreen with Apple CarPlay, for those with iPhones, and Android Auto, which made it easier for Android phone users to access their apps while driving. In some models, the seats were heated, which made the ride toasty in the dead of winter.

Jetta Dominates

Throughout the 2000s, Car and Driver magazine routinely rated the Golf as one of its 10 Best Cars. The Jetta, however, was never far behind. Jetta's latest incarnation, which debuted in 2010, was much larger and cheaper to produce than previous models, which was bad news for the competition including Toyota's Corolla, Honda's Civic, and the Nissan's Sentra. The Jetta underwent an extreme makeover in 2011, and in December 2017.

Crossovers, SUVs and Others

Volkswagen decided to enter the SUV/crossover market as the 1990s receded into history. In a crossover, the body and frame are one piece, while in a standard SUV the body is built separately and put on top of the frame. In the early 2000s, VW offered only the upscale Touareg, which in 2004 was *Motor Trend's* SUV of the year. But other SUVs, such as Honda's CR-V, routinely crushed the Touareg in sales. In 2016, the company launched the Tiguan, a mid-size 200-horsepower SUV. Engineers planned to turn the Tiguan it into a full-size SUV in 2018.

In 2017, VW unleashed its Atlas into the crowded midsize, seven passenger-seat SUV market. VW built the Atlas to compete directly with Ford's Explorer, Honda's Pilot, and the Mazda's CX-9. The Atlas was 9.5 inches longer than the Touareg and far-less expensive.

Topping out at 4,502 pounds, the Atlas needed all its six-cylinders and 276-horsepower engine to roll down the highway. With its behemoth V-6, the engine ran soft and smooth, although customers were not buying the Atlas for its fuel economy. It only got an estimated 17 miles per gallon in the city and 23 on the highway.

Other models, including the Santana, a sedan based on the second-generation Passat and named for the guitarist Carlos Santana, along with the Sagitar (a Jetta wannabe popular in China) have all been good sellers for VW, which helped make the company the world's top automaker.

What happened to New Beetle during this period? In 2012, VW dropped "New" from its name and outfitted the Bug with an improved interior and more rear room. Since then, VW has released several special Beetle editions, including the yellow and black GSR Limited and the R-Line, whose 210-horsepower engine not only increased performance, but also fuel economy, adding 1 to 2 miles per gallon.

It's Electric

During the 1950s, Volkswagen showed keen insight by opting to sell its practical Beetle in the United States. That decision helped slowly fuel the compact car craze. Still, for all its understanding of what consumers wanted, VW, unlike some other car manufacturers, lagged in the development of electric vehicles (EVs). That situation has changed in recent years as

The future is electric, believes Volkswagen. It debuted this concept "Elektro-Golf" as it built up its electric fleet.

Volkswagen reexamined the marketplace and planned its future on all-electric transportation.

It's not like the company never thought of producing EVs. On the contrary. In 1976, VW experimented with an electric Rabbit; an electrified a van , the T2 electrotransporter, and its first official electric car—the Mark I Golf. The Mark I had a 25 horsepower AC motor powered by 16 batteries. It could travel 30 miles [48.2 km] on a single charge and speed along at 60 miles per hour [96.5 km], which was not-too-shabby for an electric vehicle in those days.

The Mark I morphed into the Mark II Golf, which had a little more power. Never intended to be a car for highway use, the Mark II was marketed as a car to drive around town. VW only made 120 of them. As the years ticked by, VW tinkered with an electric Jetta and more electric Golf models.

The e-Golf debuted in Germany in 2013. It is still far from competing with the maker's bigger brands, but they have high hopes for a solid future.

In 2013, VW took its EV research to a whole new level as it introduced the e-Golf at the Frankfurt Motor Show in Germany. The company's first all-electric vehicle had a range of 83 miles [134 km]. It also got great "gas" mileage, traveling the gasoline-powered equivalent of 126 miles per gallon [203 km] in the city and 115 mpg [185 km] on the highway.

In the fall of 2016, the company unveiled an updated version. Engineers boosted the car's range from 83 miles to 124 miles [208 km] and put in an electric motor with enough horsepower and torque to accelerate from zero to 60 in 9.6 seconds. The new and improved e-Golf topped out at a speed of 93 miles an hour. It also took less time to charge.

Taking the Dive

Finally, in 2017, Volkswagen announced it was investing a whopping $10 billion over five years in developing a series of EVs that would tantalize and mesmerize consumers. That meant the EVs had to perform just as well as gasoline-powered cars, look good, and be priced competitively. The company set an ambitious goal of selling 1 million EVs by 2020.

Experts pointed out that VW's announcement was a shot across the bow of Tesla, the maker of several stylish, high-performance EVs. VW also had something more tangible to accomplish as it sought to regain its footing after the U.S. government in 2015 caught the company in an emissions testing scandal. At that time, the company admitted equipping 11 million vehicles with computer software programs that could cheat on emissions tests.

Here's a peek inside the engine and drivetrain of theAudi e-Quattro, the electric version of its popular station wagon.

The Future Today

The idea of going electric and autonomous is part of the company's TRANSFORM 2025+ program, which lays out the future of the VW brand with an emphasis on the EV market. Although some critics were skeptical, VW was adamant that it would have a staggering 25 electric car models across all its brands on the market by 2025.

Audi, a member of the Volkswagen Group, decided to take the lead in this ambitious attempt by planning to introduce its e-tron Quattro in 2018, and the upscale e-tron Sportsback in 2019. The e-tron Quattro is an all-electric SUV that uses a 90-kilowatt battery pack. It has a range of 310 miles [499 km], although many suspect the car can travel closer to 275 miles [443 km] on a single charge

ID Models

Although VW is a latecomer to electric mobility, the company's commitment to EVs can be seen in its ID series. The ID models are not only electric, but are also autonomous, which means they can drive themselves. A driver can turn on the autonomous mode whenever he or she wants. The transformation is immediate and almost magical. The steering wheel retracts seamlessly into the dashboard as the car begins to drive itself. Touch the middle of the steering boss and the steering wheel slides out again so the driver can resume driving.

In designing the conceptualized ID vehicles, engineers abandoned VW's sharp edges and embraced soft, curved front ends and rounded body shapes. Along the exterior of the cars, engineers stylishly and subtly installed cameras and sensors so each vehicle can see where it is going. The dashboard is engineered not to be flashy and fancy, but plain and non-descript with no buttons. Its covering is a sheet of fabric.

The outside and interior of a concept for the electric, autonomous ID series of cars from Volkswagen were shown off at this auto show. Will this be on the roads soon? Volkswagen's engineers and marketers are taking the pulse of the world to find out.

The ID Buzz interior shows how the car is basically autonomous. There is a steering wheel, but the vehicle is designed to run by itself without help from the "driver."

Buzz about the ID Buzz

Although Audi was taking the lead in the VW's EV revolution, Volkswagen itself planned to follow with its ID CROZZ and its ID Buzz microbus. The Buzz, fanciful and whimsical, harkens back to the "flower-power days" of the 1960s and '70s when the VW Bus was extremely popular among young people.

As early reviewers pointed out, the Buzz married mobility, independence, and environmental responsibility in an artfully designed homage to the original Bus. The Buzz has rounded edges and a front end that resembles a smiling face. From a performance standpoint, the ID Buzz can accelerate up to 99 miles an hour and hypothetically go from zero-to-60 in five seconds. A person would have to recharge its 200-kilowatt motor every 270 miles [435 km].

Yet, the Buzz is not about performance. The company hopes to tap into the nostalgia of baby boomers, those who came of age in the '60s and '70s. Still, some critics wondered whether the Buzz would make it to the showroom in 2025 knowing that VW's earlier attempts at producing EVs had been haphazard at best.

Regardless, the playful electric Buzz is much more technologically savvy than the old-style, diesel-fueled Bus. It can store on the cloud—a network of computer servers where digital information is stored—specific settings, such as seat position, air conditioning, music, and other features for both drivers and passengers. The moment a person steps into the Buzz, the vehicle will automatically adjust its settings.

The Buzz microbus is the electric version of the 1960s models that so thrilled a generation.

*The sedan version of the ID car from Volkswagen
will be called the CROZZ. Sporty, stylish, and
electric: Is it the future?*

Back inside the Buzz, this shows how the passengers can face each other while the car does the driving. The console (below) offers controls, but they are minimal.

The ultimate version of the driverless car from Volkswagen might be Sedric, which will be summoned from a smartphone app.

Headlights that Wink!

While the idea of an all-electric VW Bus might seem like a hippie's dream, VW's planned ID Crozz has headlights that wink. The lights ingeniously use colors to communicate to oncoming drivers. While the ID Buzz plays to the nostalgia of consumers, the Crozz is an electric SUV that VW hopes will appeal to a mass audience.

The company calls the Crozz its first electronically-powered crossover vehicle. Production is scheduled to begin in 2020.

Engineers designed the Crozz to be powered by an 83-kilowatt per hour lithium-ion battery and two electric motors, one on each axel. The motors can reach a healthy 302 horsepower and allow the vehicle to top out at 112 miles per hour. The Crozz's doors open electronically—sliding in the rear, and front doors that swing out at 90-degree angles.

Sedric: Driving on Its Own

Cars that drive themselves are not just the stuff of science-fiction any longer. They have become reality for such companies as Ford, Tesla, Mercedes, Google and Apple. In 2017, Volkswagen unveiled its own version of the driverless car—the Sedric.

At first glance the all-electric Sedric, which made its debut at the Geneva International Motor Show in Switzerland, looks like a cute bug (although one critic likened it to "a toaster"), perhaps in deference to the Beetle, the original "Bug."

Despite its playful appearance, whatever that may be, the car is fully autonomous, which means it performs under all roadway and environmental conditions with little or no help from a human. VW is convinced fully autonomous vehicles will make life in urban areas better.

Sedric does not have traditional brake or acceleration pedals. Nor does it have a steering wheel. Instead, a person can summon the vehicle simply by pushing a small hand-held button. The car operates by a voice-controlled AI, or artificial intelligence, "agent," much like Apple's Siri, a voice-activated assistant.

Sedric's two sliding glass doors open not to the traditional front and back seats, but to a large lounge area where passengers can enjoy a movie on the car's windscreen, which takes the place of a windshield. In fact, VW touts Sedric as a "comfortable lounge on wheels."

Humans, if they wanted to, can hold a conversation with the car as if they were friends or family. The Sedric can be programmed to do chores, such as dropping the kids off at school and picking up the groceries.

The Sedric concept

Connectivity

Thanks to the Internet and hand-held digital devices, the world has become a more connected place. In 2015, the company introduced its new "infotainment" systems on Golf models sold in the Middle East. VW equipped the cars with touch-screen technology and the opportunity to connect multiple phones using Bluetooth technology and a USB connection.

Moreover, Volkswagen has plans to install Echo, Amazon's virtual assistant, into many of its models. Drivers with VW's CarNet accounts can access Echo whose virtual assistant, Alexa, is more than eager to help. Those who currently own Amazon Echos can already command Alexa to shop for products, play music, and food for delivery.

In addition to those services, VW's Alexa-enabled cars will include many features related to the automobiles. For example, a person can ask Alexa if their car is locked or how much gas [or electricity] is left. A person can also ask Alexa to sound the horn if that person cannot find their vehicle.

If you're planning a trip from home, Alexa can help with directions and send them directly to your car. Alexa can also tell you how long it will take to get to a destination. If you're listening to music in your home, Alexa can pause it and then play the songs when you're in the car. It will also remind you to pick up dinner when you leave work, or grab the mail when you come home.

These and other technological innovations could not have been imagined when the first Beetle hit the road in the United States. In the world of Volkswagen, it seems, the future is electric, in more ways than one.

RESEARCH PROJECTS

1. Look into the early years of the Beetle and how it was used in Germany. Who drove them? How long did they last? Were they truly successful as a "people's car"?

2. Look up the annual changes in design for the Volkswagen Jetta. Make a chart comparing the years based on what exterior features changed? Why do you think they made some of the changes? Which ones were the most interesting to you?

3. Read more about autonomous cars. Make a chart of the pros and cons of such cars becoming standard on the roadways. What are the biggest benefits? What are some of the dangers? When do you think they will become a regular part of our world?

4. Become a car designer! Based on one of the models of Volkswagen in this book, sketch out your own new car that you'd like the company to make. Is it a revamped Beetle? Do you want to bring back (and improve) The Thing? Or do you have an entirely new vision for Volkswagen? Use some research and your imagination.

FIND OUT MORE

Books

Chapman, Giles. *The VW Camper Story*. Stroud, London: The History Press, 2011.

Gunnell, John. *The Complete Book of Classic Volkswagen: Beetles, Microbuses, Things, Karmann Ghias, and More*. Minneapolis, MN: Quarto Publishing, 2017.

Hajt, Jorg. *The VW Bus: History of a Passion*. Atglen, Pa.: Schiffer Publishing. 2012.

Hiott, Andrea. *Thinking Small: The Long, Strange Trip of the Volkswagen Beetle*. New York: Ballantine Books, 2012.

Web Sites

Volkswagen Official Site
www.vw.com

Car and Driver: The Bug's Life: A History of the Volkswagen Beetle
http://www.caranddriver.com/flipbook/the-bugs-life-a-history-of-the-volkswagen-beetle

BBC: Volkswagen from the Third Reich to the Emissions Scandal
http://www.bbc.com/news/business-34358783

Bloomberg: The VW Story
https://www.bloomberg.com/news/articles/2006-05-09/the-vw-storybusinessweek-business-news-stock-market-and-financial-advice

SERIES GLOSSARY OF KEY TERMS

aerodynamics the study of how air moves over and around an object

camshaft the metal rod to which pistons are attached in a car engine

chassis the metal internal framework or skeleton of a car

coupe generally used as a term for a two-door car

endurance a type of racing that is conducted over a long time period

ergonomic designed to mold or fit a person's body shape

fuel injection a process in some car engines that sends a small amount of fuel into each of the engine's many tiny combustions

grille automotive term for the front end of a car

horsepower a measurement of engine strength, based on the power that a single horse could achieve

marque a name for an automaker's logos or car models

rpm revolutions per minute, the number of times the camshaft spins in that time period

sedan typically, a four-door car

suspension the series of springs and bars that support a car while it drives

tachometer a device that measures rpms in an engine

transmission the set of gears that transfers power from the engine to the wheels of a car; in a manual transmission, the drivers moves a lever that makes the gears change; in automatic transmission, the car moves from gear to gear itself.

turbocharged describing a car engine that has additional parts that drive more air into the combustion chambers, thus increasing power of the car

INDEX

Page numbers in **boldface** type indicate photo captions.

INDEX

PHOTO CREDITS

RON KIMBALL: 4–5, 10, 16, 19, 20 (bottom), 30, 33, 40–41, 43, 47, 76, 78–79
DENIS L. TANNEY: 44, 46 (top & bottom), 48 (top & bottom), 67
VOLKSWAGEN OF AMERICA: 6, 8–9, 12, 13, 14 (bottom), 15, 17, 18 (top & bottom), 20 (top), 21 (top & bottom), 22, 23 (top & bottom),
24–25, 34 (top), 36, 38, 39, 49 (top), 50 (top & bottom), 52 (top), 59 (top & bottom), 65 (top & bottom), 66 (top & bottom), 69 (top & bottom),
70 (top & bottom), 71 (top & bottom), 73–73, 74 (top & bottom), 75 (top & bottom), 77, 86, 87, 88 top, 88 bottom, 89 top, 89 bottom, 90.
NICKY WRIGHT/NATIONAL MOTOR MUSEUM: 14 (top), 26, 28, 29, 32, 34 (bottom), 35, 49 (bottom), 51 (top & bottom), 52 (bottom),
53 (top & bottom), 54,55 (top & bottom), 56–57, 58 (top & bottom), 60 (top & bottom), 61, 62, 63 (top & bottom), 64 (top & bottom), 68
SHUTTERSTOCK: Grzegorz Czapski 80. WIKIMEDIA: Rainerhaufe 82, Clement Bucho-Lechat 83. AUDI AG MEDIA IMAGES: 84.
DREAMSTIME.COM: Mark Andrews 85T, 85B.

St Croix Falls Library
230 S Washington St
St Croix Falls WI 54024